Seasons

Words by David Bennett
Pictures by Rosalinda Kightley

Reader's Digest Kids
Pleasantville, N.Y.— Montreal

Our planet is called Earth. The earth moves around and around the sun.

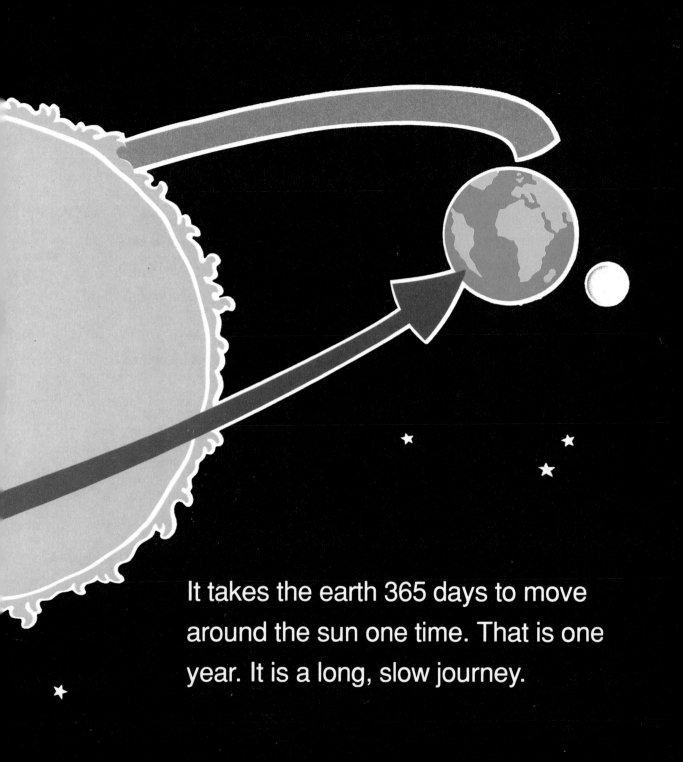

It takes the earth 365 days to move around the sun one time. That is one year. It is a long, slow journey.

During the year our weather changes. These changes are called seasons. The four seasons are:

spring

summer

all

winter

Imagine that this ball is the earth,
and the house is your home.

The earth is always tilted to one side, just like this ball. The tilt never changes.

In spring and summer, your home is tilted toward the sun. You get more light and heat at these times of year.

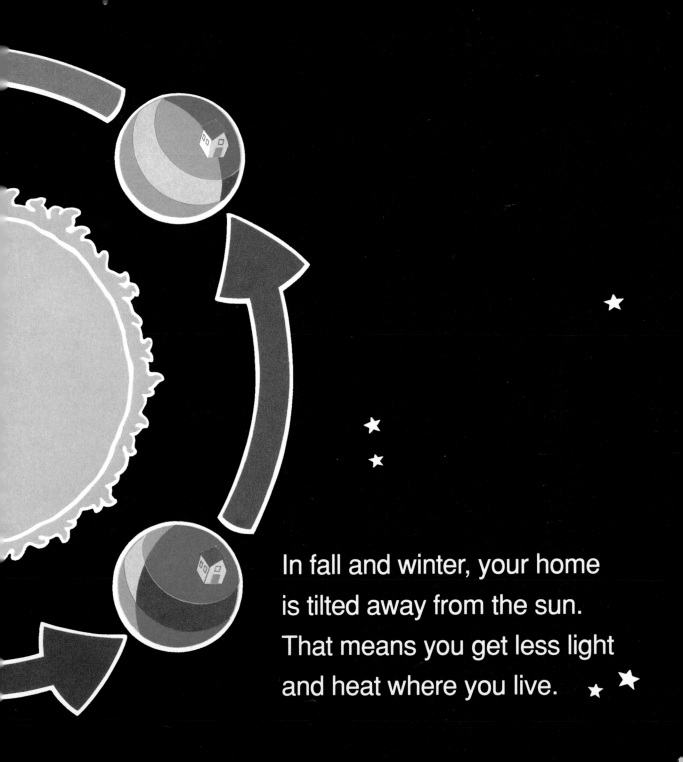

In fall and winter, your home is tilted away from the sun. That means you get less light and heat where you live.

In spring, daytime and nighttime are almost the same length. It is a bright and warm season.

Sunshine and spring rain help plants
to grow. Buds burst open on the trees,
and bulb shoots peek through the soil.

Many baby animals are born in the spring.
They will have plenty of time to grow big
and strong before the long,
cold winter season arrives.

How many baby animals can you see?

In summer, the sun looks high in the sky.
It stays light outside until quite late. You may
even go to sleep before it gets dark.

The leaves on the trees are fully open now.
Colorful flowers are everywhere.

In summer, insects munch on
leaves, and birds catch insects to
feed their young.

The sun is very strong at this time of year.

You can get a sunburn if you sit in
the sunshine too long.

As fall arrives, the sun looks lower in the sky.
The days get shorter and cooler. Leaves turn
yellow, orange, red, and brown.
Then they fall off the trees.

Most of the baby animals born in the spring can take care of themselves now.

Animals and birds eat a lot more berries and nuts in the fall. It will be difficult to find food when winter comes. Some birds fly away to warmer places to get away from the cold weather.

In winter, the days are short and the
nights are long. It gets dark very early.

Most plants rest while the weather is cold.
Many animals grow thick winter coats and
spend long hours in their homes.

It gets so cold that snow falls and covers the ground in some places. You can see where animals and birds have been walking by their footprints.

Can you see who left these footprints in the snow?

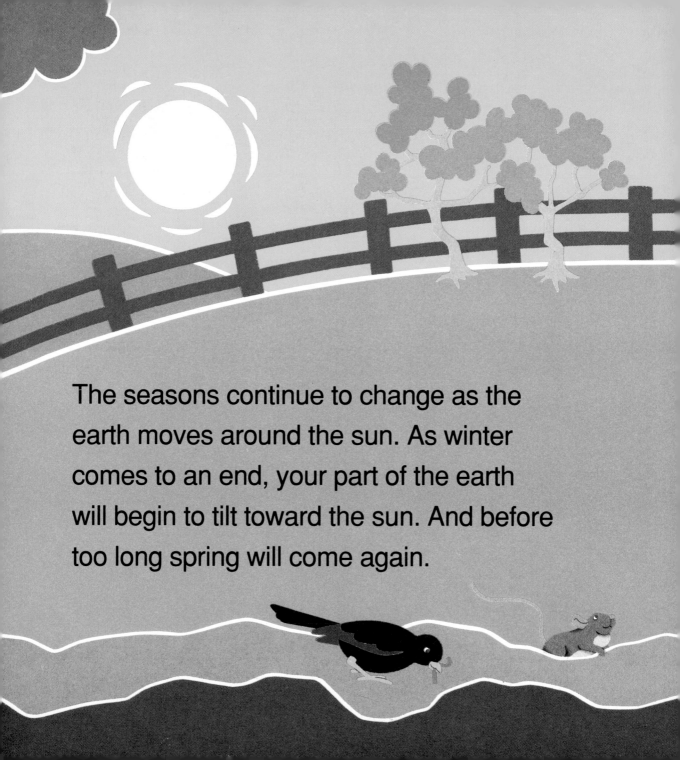

The seasons continue to change as the earth moves around the sun. As winter comes to an end, your part of the earth will begin to tilt toward the sun. And before too long spring will come again.

BEAR REVIEW

1. The earth travels around and around the sun. It takes 365 days to go around one time. That's one year.

2. The four seasons are:
   spring, summer, fall, and winter.

3. In spring and summer, the earth is tilted toward the sun. In fall and winter, the earth is tilted away from the sun.

4. The seasons continue to change as the earth moves around the sun.